Pigs

Pigs

by Christina Wilsdon

Reader's Digest

Published by The Reader's Digest Association, Inc.
London • New York • Sydney • Montreal

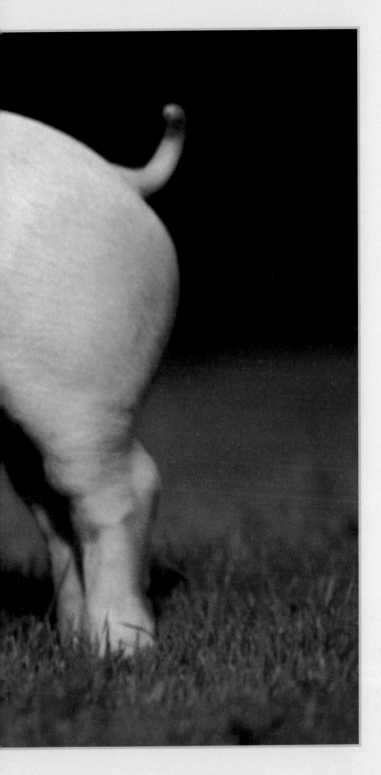

CONTENTS

Chapter 1

A pig story

wild WORDS

boar   a male pig.

sow   a female pig that has had babies.

piglet   a baby pig .

litter   a family of piglets.

Bundles of joy

A sow can have as many as 12 babies at a time. Some kinds of pigs have 15 or more. A few pigs have given birth to more than 30 piglets in one litter! The piglets born first start drinking their mother's milk even before their younger brothers and sisters are born.

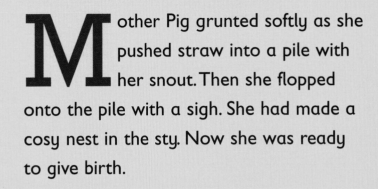

Mother Pig grunted softly as she pushed straw into a pile with her snout. Then she flopped onto the pile with a sigh. She had made a cosy nest in the sty. Now she was ready to give birth.

The baby pigs arrived quickly — all 12 of them! They crowded against Mother Pig's belly, along which were two rows of teats, which held milk. The teats near Mother Pig's front legs offered the most milk, so the baby pigs fought to get there. They shoved and jostled each other, pushing hard with their snouts and hoofs.

Soon the strongest baby pigs won the best places. They began to drink. Further along their mother's belly, the other piglets also settled down to feed. Mother Pig grunted contentedly as she nursed them.

After all that work, it was time for a nap. The piglets snuggled up in the straw. A heat lamp provided extra warmth for them.

Baby Pig was the biggest piglet of all. He fought his way to the spot where he could get the best of Mother Pig's milk. And he was the first of the litter to take a look outside his home.

More pigs lived nearby in other pig arks — modern-style pig homes — scattered across a big field. The pigs were free to go in and out of them. But for now, the baby pigs stayed in a little fenced yard next to their home.

The little yard was filled with straw. Baby Pig loved to dig in the straw and push it around with his snout.

Baby Pig also played with his brothers and sisters. They scampered and leaped about. They nipped at each other and pushed each other over.

The farmer gave the baby pigs special toys to keep them busy as some piglets get restless and may injure each other. He hung up a chain and pieces of plastic pipe in the pen. Baby Pig liked to play with the chain.

When playtime was over, Baby Pig and most of his brothers and sisters flopped down into a pink pile to nap. The others stayed with Mother Pig.

At first Baby Pig's only food was his mother's milk. But when he was about a week old, the farmer began giving the piglets their own special feed, called 'creep food', which consisted of fine pellets high in vegetable protein to help them to grow.

This little piggy…

Sometimes a litter of piglets includes tiny babies that are only half the size of the others. A piglet that is very small is called a runt. A runt may be too weak and small to get its fair share of milk. Runts are often removed from the litter and raised separately.

Baby Pig grew fast. He weighed about 2.5kg when he was born. Now, at the age of five weeks, he weighed nearly 7kg. The baby pigs were old enough to go outside with Mother Pig. They rooted in the dirt in search of good things to eat. They ran and played, squealing and oinking. On warm days, they lay in cool dirt or mud. They huddled in straw inside their hut when it was chilly.

The farmer visited the pigs every day. Baby Pig liked it when the farmer scratched him on his back. It felt so much better than when he scratched his own back against a fence post.

By the time he is six months old, Baby Pig will be half the size of Mother Pig. He will probably weigh about 100kg – as much as a newborn baby elephant.

Chapter 2

The body of a pig

A sow lets her piglets nurse
for six to ten weeks after
their birth. After that, she
will push them away.

Pick a pig

There are about 500 breeds of domestic pigs. Some have long, lean bodies. Others are plump and round. But all pigs look a bit like barrels with legs. Each leg has four toes, but the pig walks only on the middle two. Its toes are called hoofs, just like the toes of cows and other hoofed animals.

Skin, hair and colour

A pig's skin is thick but sensitive. A white-skinned pig can easily get sunburnt. A pig can also get too hot very quickly as it does not sweat to cool off like a human does. It must soak itself in a puddle or mud hole instead.

Bristly hair grows out of a pig's skin. Pigs that live in the wild have longer, thicker hair than farm pigs. A few kinds of pig have hardly any hair at all.

Many pigs are pink but can also be black, white, brown, red, red-yellow and blue-grey, or a mixture of colours.

Some kinds of pigs always have certain patterns. Oxford Sandy and Black pigs or Gloucester Old Spot pigs are both white with black spots or patches, while Saddlebacks have a white band around their shoulders and front legs.

Pigs' eyes and ears

A pig has small eyes and can't see well. But it has a good sense of hearing. Some breeds have short, perky ears that stick up. Others have long ears that droop. Some have extra-long, extra-droopy ears called lop ears.

About snouts

A pig's nose is called a snout. At the end of the snout is a rubbery pad with a pair of nostrils. This pad is as sensitive to touch as a human's hand. A pig uses its strong and flexible snout to dig around in dirt and feel for things to eat as it snuffles across the ground. Its sense of smell is also very sharp. A pig can smell buried food from a distance of 6m – that would be a bit like you being able to smell what is in a closed lunchbox across a room!

Noisy oinkers

Pigs can be noisy. They oink, grunt and snort. They squeal when they are excited or scared. Scientists have measured a pig's squeal and found that it was louder than the music at a rock concert!

Pigs make a variety of different sounds – oinks, grunts, snorts and also squeals.

19

Pigs sometimes wag their tails as they drink their mother's milk or eat from a trough.

A pig's tail

Pigs that live in the wild have straight tails. Farm pigs have curly tails, but they can uncurl them. A relaxed pig may let its tail hang down. An alert pig curls its tail and holds it up on its back.

Baby pigs often bite one another's tails when they play or fight. Sometimes farmers shorten piglets' tails to stop them from hurting each other.

Big pigs, little pigs

All piglets grow quickly, but different kinds of pigs grow up to be different sizes. Some kinds of farm pigs weigh 180kg to 225kg when they are fully grown. That's about as much as a pony. Other pigs grow even larger and weigh more than 270kg!

DID YOU KNOW?

The biggest pig on record was a Poland China hog named **Big Bill**. He weighed 1,158kg – twice the weight of most of his breed and more than some small motor cars – and measured nearly 3m from snout to tail.

Chapter 3

What pigs do

A pig pushes and snuffles its snout around in the dirt or any kind of groundcover to look for food. Pig farmers call this rooting.

24

Pigging out

Have you ever heard someone say, 'Stop eating like a pig'? A person who eats like a pig is eating too much or eating sloppily – or both!

Pigs do eat sloppily. But pigs do not tend to overeat. They eat only what they need. That is different from a horse, which will eat until it is sick if it can get into the room where its food is kept!

A pig growing up on a pig farm eats from 2.5kg to 3.6kg of food a day. Its meals include grains such as corn and wheat. Pigs may also eat a special pelleted pig feed made from grains and mixed with vitamins, minerals and proteins. A pig raised by a family may get leftovers from the table as well.

A pig that is allowed to root in the dirt outdoors finds other tasty titbits. It eats the same things that pigs in the wild eat – roots, seeds, leaves, fruits, nuts, mushrooms and even worms, insects, slugs, snails and mice!

In France, pigs are specially trained to root out a highly prized and expensive type of fungus called a 'truffle' but the farmer has to be very quick to grab the truffle before the pig can eat it!

Pigs at rest

A farm pig spends about 2 hours a day eating. A pig in the wild spends about 7 hours a day eating because it must work harder to find food.

What does a pig do with the rest of its time? Mostly, it sleeps! A pig sleeps from 11 to 13 hours a day. This sounds like a lot, but it is a mere nap compared to a cat or lion that sleeps about 18 hours a day! A sleepy pig flops down on its side to snooze, and even its curly tail relaxes.

Pigs at play

Pigs are clever animals. They can even learn tricks easily. Scientists have found that pigs are as clever as cats and dogs, if not cleverer.

Pigs that can go outdoors find plenty to do. They spend lots of time rooting in the dirt. But pigs that are raised indoors in pens can get bored. They may bite each other if they do not have something better to do.

So farmers give indoor pigs plenty of hay so that they have something to root in. They may also hang sections of rubber hose over the pen for pigs to chew and tug on.

Pigs will flop down and stretch out to take a nap anytime, anywhere.

Wallowing in mud keeps a pig cool and protects its skin from sunburn and biting insects.

28

Mud baths

Pigs are famous for being dirty, but they are actually clean animals. A pig in a pen keeps its home cleaner than a horse or cow does. It sleeps in one area and goes to the bathroom in a different area. It will not play with a ball or other toy that has manure on it.

What about all the pictures of pigs in mud puddles? A pig taking a mud bath is not trying to get dirty. It is trying to keep cool, because it does not have sweat glands that would enable it to sweat to cool off. It must use water outside its body to cool down.

A pig prefers to choose a clean, damp patch of dirt or a puddle of water if it can. It will soak in mud only if that is all there is. Spending time in a puddle or a mud hole is called wallowing.

When necessary, electric fans are used to cool off pigs that live indoors. In hot countries farmers may also use fine-mist sprinklers or, if they have just a few pigs, they may spray them down with a garden hose.

Show-stoppers!

Pigs are sometimes shown at agricultural shows and other events. The pigs are judged on their overall appearance. Their owners scrub the pigs until they are squeaky clean. They even shave the hair from the pigs' ears and tails to make them look extra tidy.

Chapter 4

Pigs in the wild

The wild boar is the 'great-granddaddy', or ancestor, of most kinds of farm pigs.

What a boar!

Most pigs are farm pigs. But some pigs still root and grunt in the wild. One of these wild pigs is the wild boar.

A wild boar is not fat and round like a farm pig. It has long legs and strong shoulders. Thick, bristly black or brown hair covers its body. Two of its upper teeth grow up and out of its mouth. These teeth are called tusks. Tusks may be 7.5cm to 13cm long but sometimes grow as big as bananas! Two lower teeth stick out of a boar's mouth, too.

Wild boar once lived only in Europe, Asia and part of Africa. But people in the past brought wild boar to almost every land they visited. They set them free so that they would have boars to hunt when they needed food. Wild boar probably became extinct in Britain in the 13th century but were reintroduced in later centuries. Captive boar are now kept in British wildlife parks and bred on farms but – thanks to escapes and deliberate releases – a few hundred are now again living here in the wild.

Wild boar can survive in woods and fields as well as rain forests and dry places near deserts. Their favourite foods are nuts and acorns. They also eat fruit, insects, worms, lizards, eggs, mice – and even baby deer!

Baby boar

Baby boar have attractive brown-and-tan striped fur. The stripes protect the young boar by helping them to blend in with plants. This blending into the background is called camouflage. The young boar lose their stripes when they are about 3 months old.

Bumps on a hog

The warthog is a distant cousin of wild boars and farm pigs. It lives in the grasslands of Africa. This pig gets its name from its face, which sprouts four big bumps. These bumps are very big on a male warthog's face. They help to protect him when he fights with other male warthogs.

A warthog can run up to 35 miles per hour. That's faster than a car driving on a city street. It needs this speed to run away from lions, leopards and cheetahs, which are the warthog's main predators. The warthog holds its tail straight up in the air when it runs.

Warthogs eat mainly grass. They kneel down on their front legs to graze. They do not usually root for food as farm pigs do. They can also tolerate hotter weather than farm pigs can. But warthogs will gladly wallow in mud whenever they get the chance!

Warthogs sleep in underground dens. Usually the den is an old burrow that was made by another animal. If a warthog can't find an old den, it may dig out a hollow under a bush.

A warthog will also hide from danger in its den and always goes into the den tail first. That way, any animal that dares to enter its den will meet a face full of sharp tusks!

Both male and female warthogs have tusks. An old male's tusks may grow to be as long as a 30cm ruler!

Hog wild

Some feral pigs look a lot like wild boars. Others look like a cross between a boar and a farm pig.

In other countries, there are populations of pigs that run free in woods, forests and fields. These are often not really members of a wild species, or kind, of pig. They are simply descended from pigs that escaped from farms and are called feral pigs. Runaway pigs survive very well in the wild because they eat so many kinds of foods.

Feral pigs are a problem in many places. Pigs root to find food. Their wallowing makes puddles and mud holes larger. Rooting and wallowing destroy the plants that grow in these spots. Then there are no roots to hold the soil in place. When rain falls, the soil washes away.

Feral pigs also eat the roots of plants, killing them. This makes it easier for weeds to grow. Then the weeds take over the soil and leave no room for other kinds of plants. Without the plants, other wild animals in the area do not have the food and shelter they need.

In Hawaii, feral pigs have damaged many wild areas. They have turned parts of rain forests into weedy, muddy patches. Mosquitoes come to lay eggs in these wet patches, spreading a disease that has killed many Hawaiian birds. Building fences and hunting are two ways people control feral pigs.

Chapter 5

Pigs and people

There are almost one billion farm pigs in the world today.

Hog history

The world's first wild pigs lived about 40 million years ago – long after the last dinosaurs died out.

About 9,000 years ago, people started to tame pigs and rear them for food. Over time, the farm pigs became different from wild pigs in many ways. They looked different and were tamer. An animal that goes through changes like this is called a domesticated animal.

Pigs were probably first domesticated in the Middle East. Not long after, pigs were also domesticated in China.

Pigs as pork

Almost half of the world's tens of millions of farm pigs are raised in China. There are about 4.9 million pigs in the UK. Pigs are farmed for their meat, called pork – pork chops, bacon, ham and pork sausages all come from pigs.

Other parts of pigs are used in different ways. Pigskin is made into shoes, gloves and other clothing. Hog hair is used to make bristles for brushes. Even the pig's fat, blood and bones are used. It is sometimes said that when it comes to pigs, you can use 'everything but the oink'!

Working pigs and pets

A pig's hearty appetite can make it useful. In past times, pigs were allowed to wander freely in villages to clean up rotting produce and other rubbish. Farmers also let pigs root in the fields as they ate weeds and helped to turn over the soil. And for centuries, farmers in France and Italy have used pigs to sniff out rare, tasty truffles.

People who keep pigs as pets often choose Vietnamese pot-bellied pigs – named for their round, low-slung tummies. They have short legs, short noses and wrinkly skin. These pigs can be trained to use a litter box like a cat and can learn tricks, too.

FAST FACTS ABOUT THE FARM PIG

SCIENTIFIC NAME	*Sus scrofa domesticus*
CLASS	Mammals
ORDER	Artiodactyla
SIZE	Males up to 1.8m in length, depending on breed
WEIGHT	68kg-680kg, depending on breed and age
HEIGHT	0.3m-1.2m, depending on breed
LIFE SPAN	Up to 21 years
HABITAT	Farms

DID YOU KNOW?

Some of the pig's wild cousins are rare. The rarest is the pygmy hog, which lives in a part of India. This tiny pig weighs only 6kg to 10kg – about as much as a six-week-old farm piglet! The pygmy hog is rare because there is not much left of the vast grasslands where it once roamed.

Vietnamese pot-bellied pigs can be great family pets. They are affectionate and quite easy to train.

GLOSSARY OF *wild* WORDS

boar	an adult male pig
breeds	different varieties of the same animal species
domesticated	animals that have been bred over time to be tame companions and farm animals
feral	domestic animals that are no longer tame and live in the wild

hog	a male pig that is especially raised for food
litter	a family of piglets
piglet	a baby pig
pork	meat from pigs
predator	an animal that hunts and eats other animals to survive

root	to push around and dig in dirt using the snout	species	a group of living things that are the same in many ways
snout	the part of an animal's head where the nose and jaws stick out in front	tusk	a very long, pointed tooth that sticks far out from the side of an animal's mouth – usually one of a pair
snuffle	to breathe in to smell something		
sow	an adult female pig that has had piglets	wallow	to lie in water or mud to cool off

INDEX

CREDITS

Pigs is an ***All About Animals*** fact book
Written by Christina Wilsdon

Published in 2010 in the United Kingdom by Vivat Direct Limited (t/a Reader's Digest),
157 Edgware Road, London W2 2HR

Editor: Rachel Warren Chadd
Designer: Nicola Liddiard
Art editor: Simon Webb

Printed and bound in Europe by Arvato Iberia

ISBN: 978 0 276 44614 6
Book code: 640-023 UP0000-1
Oracle code: 504500025H.00.24